TEMPERATURE

by Brenda Walpole
Illustrations by Dennis Tinkler
Photographs by Chris Fairclough

Contents

Gareth Stevens Publishing
MILWAUKEE

Hot and cold

Hot and *cold* are words we often use in our daily lives to describe the "temperature" of something. Is it hot or cold outside today? What are your favorite hot and cold foods?

You can often decide whether something is likely to be hot or cold just by looking at it. Can you tell which place in these two photographs is hot and which is cold? How did you make your decision?

It is important to decide whether something is likely to be hot or cold because it can help prevent accidents. When you see a cup of cocoa, you know it is likely to be hot. This stops you from burning your tongue. You know ice cream will feel cold in your mouth. But you can't actually "see" how hot or cold things are. You must sip your cocoa carefully and check that it's not too hot. And before you get into the bathtub, you feel the water with your hand to find out how hot or cold it is.

Sometimes we need to know precisely the "hotness" or "coldness" of something. This means we need to measure its temperature. Meteorologists determine the exact temperature of the air outside. Doctors measure the body temperature of their patients in order to find out if they are sick.

Feel the heat

Nerves in our skin sense the temperature of our surroundings. We feel warm close to a fire because heat from the fire reaches our bodies and increases the temperature of our skin. In a cold place, we lose some of our body heat and begin to feel chilly.

What we are doing or wearing can make us feel hot or cold. Even on a cold, snowy day, you can feel warm if you are warmly dressed and running around.

Feel a change in temperature

You will need:
three small bowls; very warm, cold, and tepid water; a watch.

Fill one bowl with very warm water, the second with cold water, and the third with tepid water. Dip your left hand into the cold water and your right hand into the very warm water. Leave them there for about one minute. Then dip both hands into the tepid water.

Does the tepid water feel warm or cool to your left hand?
Does it feel the same to your right hand?

When the temperature drops suddenly, it takes us a while to adjust to the change.

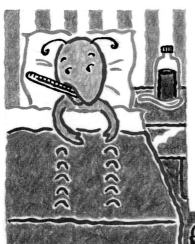

Sometimes we need to measure temperature exactly. When cooking, it's important to be aware of changes in temperature, but the stove gets far too hot for us to touch. Meteorologists who study the weather need to compare the precise temperatures of different places. When you are sick, it is important to know exactly what your body temperature is and whether or not it changes. To measure all of these things, we use different kinds of thermometers.

Measuring temperature

A thermometer has a scale. We use the scale on a thermometer to measure different temperatures.

Something to try

Make your own thermometer

You will need: a thin plastic straw, a tall glass bottle, food coloring, modeling clay, a pen, a strip of cardboard, clear tape, a measuring cup.

Color 6 ounces (170 milliliters) of water with food coloring. Pour the colored water into the bottle. Place the straw in the bottle so one end is just below the surface of the liquid. Hold it at this level by plugging the neck of the bottle with clay. Then seal the end of the straw that is sticking out of the bottle with clay so everything is airtight. To make a scale, tape the cardboard onto the bottle, and mark the level of the liquid in the straw. This mark on the cardboard scale is your room temperature. Now stand the bottle in a bowl of warm water. After about two minutes, mark on your scale the new level of the liquid in the straw.

With the help of an adult, now stand your "thermometer" in a bowl of very hot water. As the liquid in the straw gets hotter, it will rise higher. Mark the new level on your scale. Remove your thermometer. The liquid in the straw will return to its original level as it cools.

P.S. Try this experiment using a real thermometer to measure temperature. Mark your scale in degrees Fahrenheit or Celsius.

6

Thermometers show changes in temperature. When the liquid inside the thermometer becomes warm, it expands. Then the liquid fills more of the tube, just as the water in your thermometer rose up the straw.

People in the United States usually measure temperature on the Fahrenheit scale in units called degrees Fahrenheit (°F). On this scale, 32°F is the temperature at which pure water freezes, and 212°F is the temperature at which it boils. Most everyday temperatures fall within this range, but not all.

The metric system, however, uses a Celsius scale (also called centigrade) in which water freezes at 0°C and boils at 100°C. An international agreement in 1948 named this scale of measuring temperature after a Swedish astronomer, Anders Celsius.

Look at the illustration of the thermometer. Can you read the temperature on it? Do you think this temperature is the right one for any of the pictures? What temperature do you think would be appropriate for each picture?

desert
temperature

boiling point
of water

hummingbird's
temperature

body temperature

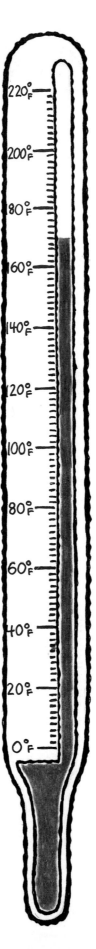

220°F
200°F
80°F
60°F
140°F
120°F
100°F
80°F
60°F
40°F
20°F
0°F

freezing point
of water

autumn day

summer day

Early thermometers

Early thermometers contained both liquid and air. When air gets warm, it expands, and when it cools, it contracts, or shrinks, just like liquid. The device shown in the photograph is called a thermoscope. It was developed by the Italian scientist Galileo and was used at the end of the sixteenth century. The picture below shows how the thermoscope worked. The thermoscope had a glass flask with a long, thin neck that was filled with colored water or alcohol. When the temperature fell, the air in the bulb at the top contracted, making the liquid in the flask rise up the tube to fill the space.

air

When the temperature falls, the air contracts, and the liquid goes up.

When the temperature rises, the air expands, and the liquid goes down.

glass flask

colored liquid

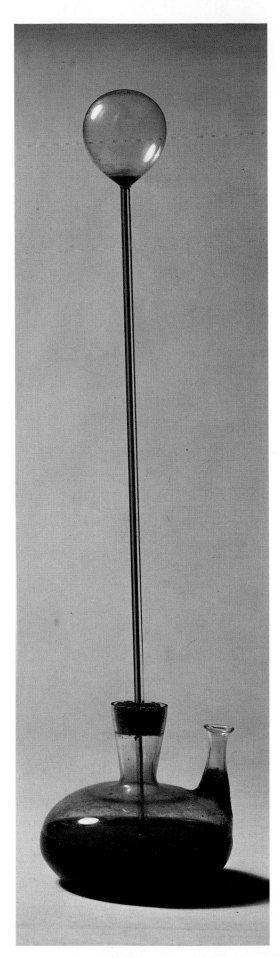

In 1660, Otto von Guericke, a German scientist, had this large air-thermometer on the wall of his house in Magdeburg. But air-filled thermometers are not very accurate because they are affected by air pressure as well as the temperature outside the thermometer. In 1654, Ferdinand II, Grand Duke of Tuscany, invented the first sealed thermometer that contained liquid. Sealed thermometers are more reliable because they are not affected by air pressure.

As thermometers became more accurate, scientists tried to agree on a standard measuring scale that could be divided into degrees of temperature. All kinds of things were suggested as a starting point — the melting point of butter, the temperature of blood, and even the temperature of the cellar in the Paris Observatory. Eventually, the freezing and boiling points of water were chosen as two standard points on the scale.

In 1717, a Dutch instrument-maker named G. D. Fahrenheit began making mercury-filled thermometers. His Fahrenheit scale set the freezing point of water at 32°F and its boiling point at 212°F. This temperature scale is widely used in the United States and by some people in Britain, although the Celsius scale is favored by scientists.

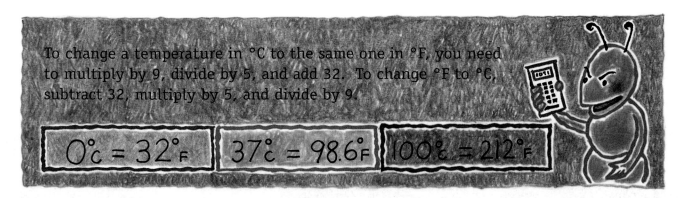

To change a temperature in °C to the same one in °F, you need to multiply by 9, divide by 5, and add 32. To change °F to °C, subtract 32, multiply by 5, and divide by 9.

0°C = 32°F   37°C = 98.6°F   100°C = 212°F

Modern thermometers

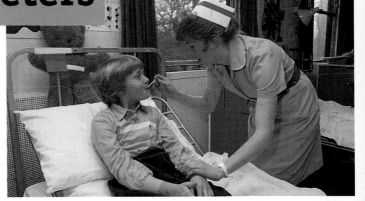

Many different kinds of thermometers are used today. They often have special features for particular jobs. A clinical thermometer, used to measure body temperature, has a narrow section in the tube that stops the mercury from going back to the bulb until it is shaken. The doctor or nurse then has time to read the patient's temperature.

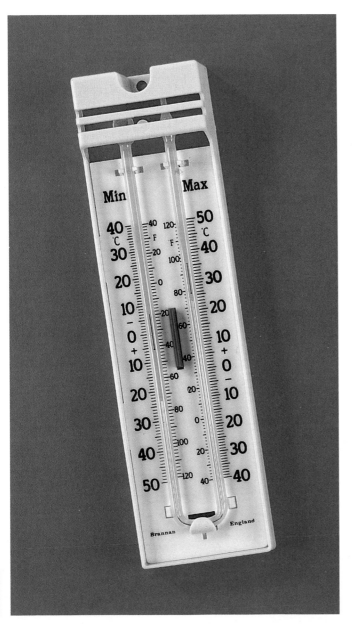

Some thermometers contain different liquids to measure extreme temperatures. In the Arctic, where the temperature can fall to -58°F (-50°C), mercury thermometers cannot be used because the mercury freezes at -38°F (-39°C). Since alcohol freezes at a lower temperature than mercury, alcohol is used in cold weather thermometers. But alcohol boils in very hot water, so a mercury thermometer is used to measure high temperatures.

A maximum-and-minimum thermometer is used to measure the highest and lowest temperatures reached over a period of time. This kind of thermometer is really made from two different thermometers. One contains mercury and the other alcohol. Each thermometer also contains a tiny piece of metal that is wedged into the tube. In the mercury thermometer, the piece of metal is pushed upward ahead of the mercury. Because it is so tightly wedged into the tube, it doesn't fall back down again once the mercury drops down. So the piece of metal in the mercury thermometer works as a marker and shows the highest temperature reached. In the alcohol thermometer, the piece of metal marks the lowest temperature reached.

The thermometer has to be reset each day, using a magnet to pull the metal markers back to their original positions.

A thermocouple is a very up-to-date thermometer that measures temperature using electricity. A thermocouple contains two wires made of different metals that are connected to an electric current measurer called an ammeter. This picture shows a man making a thermocouple. He is welding the two metal wires together.

As the two different metals in the thermometer are heated, they react differently, and the electric current flowing through them changes. The ammeter measures this change and uses this information to record a change in temperature very precisely. The temperature is shown on a scale.

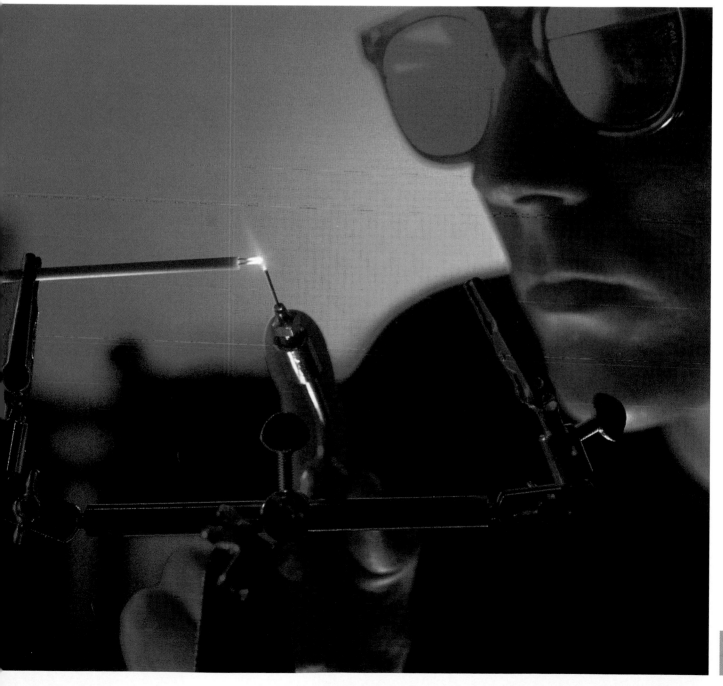

Temperature all around us

During the day, as the Sun moves across the sky, the temperature outside changes. When the Sun is high in a clear sky, its rays shine directly down to warm us. Sometimes clouds stop some of the Sun's heat from reaching the ground. Wind also has a cooling effect because fast-moving air carries heat away. Shady areas are always cooler than those in direct sunlight.

This engraving from about 1800, of the Observatory of Montsouris in France, shows meteorologists with an instrument that measured the heat given off by the Sun.

Something to try

Keep a temperature diary

On a sunny day, take the temperature of your school playground once an hour throughout the day. Make a chart of your results. What is the hottest part of the day?

P.S. Repeat the experiment on a cloudy day. Are there any differences? Can you explain them?

The hottest parts of Earth are near the Equator, where the Sun's rays are strongest. Places near the Equator receive the full force of the Sun's rays all the time. Other parts of Earth receive the Sun's rays at an angle, rather than directly. These places get less heat from the Sun. Also, as Earth rotates, some parts of it are turned away from the Sun for long periods of time. The coldest places on Earth are the North and South poles.

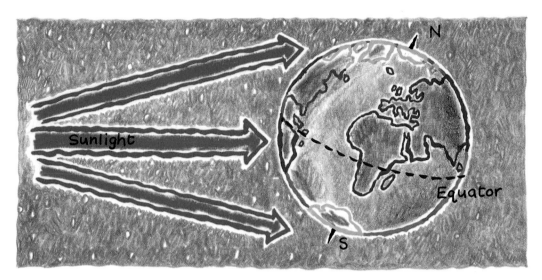

Earth is surrounded by a layer of gases called the atmosphere. Our atmosphere traps warmth from the Sun and keeps Earth's temperature fairly constant. On the Moon, there is no atmosphere, and the temperature varies widely. At night, it can be as low as -238°F (-150°C), but during the day, when the Sun beats down, it can be over 212°F (100°C).

The average temperature on Mars is -4°F (-20°C). On Venus it is a roasting 896°F (480°C), while the surface of the Sun has a temperature of approximately 9,932°F (5,500°C).

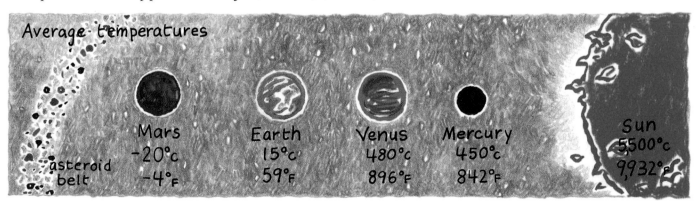

Average temperatures

| asteroid belt | Mars -20°c -4°F | Earth 15°c 59°F | Venus 480°c 896°F | Mercury 450°c 842°F | Sun 5,500°c 9,932°F |

Record-breakers

The hottest recorded temperature on Earth is 134°F (56.7°C) in Death Valley, California. The coldest temperature is -128.5°F (-89.2°C) in Vostok, Antarctica.

Hot air

On warm days, the Sun heats up the land, which then heats the air above it. Warm air rises because it is lighter than cold air. When cooler, heavier air moves in to replace the rising air, we feel a breeze. Air moves around the atmosphere like this all the time, warming up and cooling down, rising and falling. High above us, air currents called thermals are created by the rising and falling air. Glider pilots use these currents to lift their gliders high into the air.

During the day, land heats up more quickly than bodies of water, such as oceans or lakes. Warm air rises from the land, and cooler air from the water creates a breeze. At night, land cools down quicker than water, and the breeze blows in the opposite direction.

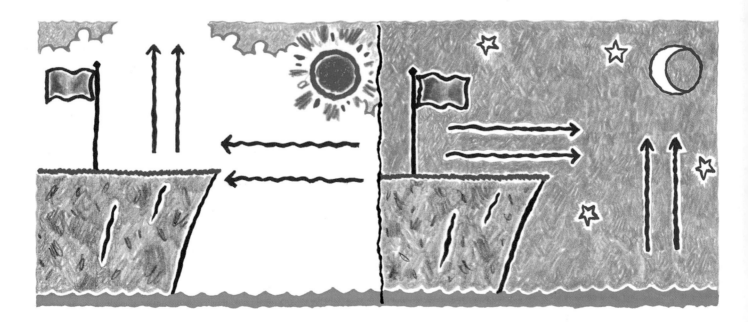

Sometimes, if you put your hand just above a radiator, you can feel the warm air rising. The radiator heats the air above it, and this lighter air rises. You can see the effect of moving air by making and using a radiator snake.

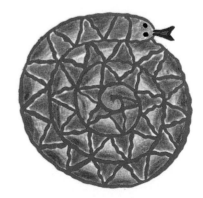

Make a radiator snake

You will need: paper, scissors, colored pencils, a thumbtack, a needle, a length of thread, a ruler, a compass.

Make a spiral design starting with a circle 8 inches (20.3 centimeters) in diameter. Decorate it with bright colors and cut it out. Use the tack to make a tiny hole, and then pull the thread through the snake's tail. Hang it above the radiator so it can twirl freely.

Hot-air balloons rise because of the hot, light air inside them. In 1783, Jacques-Etienne and Joseph-Michel Montgolfier built the first hot-air balloon that was able to carry a person. The air inside the balloon was heated by fire. The air in modern balloons is heated by gas burners carried in the basket.

Heating solid objects

Heat can travel through solid objects. We can't see heat moving, but we can measure the temperature change of an object that has been heated. Heat doesn't travel through all materials at the same speed.

Something to try

See how fast heat travels

You will need: a plastic spoon, a metal spoon, a Popsicle stick, a nail, a bowl of hot water, a watch, a friend, an adult.

Ask an adult to fill a small bowl with hot water. Dip one end of the metal spoon in the water, letting go when the end you are holding becomes hot. Get a friend to write down how long this takes. Then do the same with the plastic spoon, Popsicle stick, and nail. Which objects get hot most quickly?

P.S. How can you make sure this is an accurate test?

Metal carries heat quickly, and its temperature soon rises. We call materials like these good conductors of heat. Wood and plastic are poor conductors of heat.

Most saucepans are made of metal, which conducts heat well and allows the food inside to heat up quickly. Old-fashioned saucepans were all metal. Now, many saucepan handles are made of wood or plastic, which does not become hot. This makes the handles safer to hold.

When objects become hotter, they expand. Steel girders in bridges expand when the temperature rises. The Forth Railway Bridge in Scotland is more than 1 yard (meter) longer in summer than in winter.

You can loosen a tight metal lid on a jar by holding it under warm water a few moments. The heat makes the metal expand more than the glass, and then the cap can be unscrewed easily.

Insulation

An insulator is a material that does not let heat pass through it easily. Wood and plastic are good insulators, as you discovered with the spoon test on page 16. Air is another very good insulator that can help prevent heat traveling from a warm place to a cooler one.

Home insulation, such as the type shown in this attic, stops heat from escaping. This helps us heat our homes more efficiently, saving both money and the world's fuel resources.

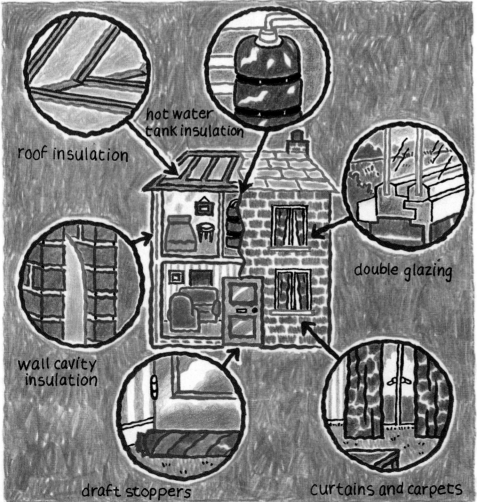

roof insulation

hot water tank insulation

double glazing

wall cavity insulation

draft stoppers

curtains and carpets

The illustration at the left shows some of the different types of insulation we use in our homes.

We use many different materials as insulators, but they all contain tiny pockets of air. Our clothes keep us warm. Several layers of clothes are warmer than one because each layer traps a layer of insulating air.

Insulation can also be used to keep cold things cold.
Sometimes cold drinks are kept cool in thermal cups.
All refrigerators and freezers have layers of insulation
in their walls.

See how heat can be kept in

You will need:
four identical
plastic cups with
lids, a thermometer,
newspaper, cotton
or woolen fabric,
aluminum foil,
a measuring cup,
warm water, a watch,
paper, a pen.

Fill all the cups to the same level with warm water. Take the
temperature inside each cup and put a lid on each cup. Then
insulate each one in a different way. Wrap the first in newspaper, the second in fabric, and the third in foil. Leave one
cup and lid unwrapped. At three-minute intervals, take the
temperature of the water in each cup again. Make a chart of
your results. Which cup keeps the water warm for the longest
time? Which material seems to be the best insulator?

P.S. Put an ice cube on a plate.
Use different kinds of insulators
to cover the cube. How long can
you keep the cube frozen?

Your body temperature

Something to try

Take your temperature over a day

Take your own temperature with a clinical thermometer. The thermometer should read about 98.6°F (37°C). But it may be half a degree or so above or below this temperature. Your body temperature is lowest in the early hours of the morning and slightly higher in the evening. Try taking your temperature at different times of the day. Take your temperature when you are in a cold place and when you are somewhere very warm. Does it change or stay the same? What is your own average temperature?

Your body works best at about 98.6°F (37°C). Usually your body controls your temperature automatically, keeping it at a healthy level. When you are cold, you may shiver. As you shiver, your muscles move and make extra heat. This warms you up. When you are too hot, you may sweat. The sweat evaporates, or dries, and cools down the surface of your skin.

When water evaporates on the skin, it takes heat from the body. That's why you may feel cold when you first get out of a bath or swimming pool. As soon as you have dried the evaporating water from your body, you will stop losing heat and feel warmer.

P.S. Roll up your sleeves and sprinkle one arm with water. Wave both arms slowly out in the air. As the wet arm dries, notice how each arm feels.

A high body temperature is a sign that you may be sick. Your temperature rises as you fight infections that make you ill. If a person is exposed to very cold temperatures, the body temperature may fall to a dangerously low level. This is called hypothermia.

21

Blood temperature

Some animals are able to control their body temperature, keeping it at roughly the same level all the time. These animals are said to be warm-blooded. All birds and mammals, including humans, are warm-blooded. When it is cold, birds can fluff up their feathers to trap a warm layer of insulating air around them. Many birds line their nests with feathers to keep their eggs warm. In winter, some warm-blooded animals hibernate. They avoid the cold weather, and, because they are not active for long periods of time, they need to use less energy.

During hot weather, some mammals cool down by sweating and panting. Furry animals stop themselves from becoming too hot by shedding their fur, or molting. After shedding, their fur lies closer to their bodies. This means less air is trapped as an insulating layer around their bodies. This keeps them cooler, as well.

Most animals, including fish, reptiles, and insects, are cold-blooded, which means they do not control their body temperatures in the same way as warm-blooded animals. The body temperature of a cold-blooded animal changes with its surroundings.

When it is cold, crocodiles and lizards don't move much, but they do come out to bask in warm sunshine to soak up the heat. On cool days, butterflies flap their wings to warm themselves up before they fly.

Both cold-blooded and warm-blooded animals can become overheated. In the midday sun, desert animals often hide in the shade. They move around most in the early morning and evening, which is when the air is cooler.

Many animals behave in certain ways to help them keep warm or cool. Penguins stand together in groups, protecting the birds in the center from freezing winds. When the birds on the outside get cold, they change places with the birds at the center.

Temperature and growth

Some living things will grow faster in warm conditions. We plant seeds in a temperature-controlled greenhouse to help them germinate, or sprout, and to help the plants grow more quickly.

Make your own greenhouse

You will need: an empty, flat plastic container; waxed paper; a packet of seeds; a glass jar; water.

Use the container to make a seed tray. Line the bottom with waxed paper and sprinkle the seeds on it. Cover one area of seeds with an upturned glass jar and leave the seeds to grow in a sunny place. Don't forget to water the seeds regularly. Which seeds germinate first? Which grow larger?

Yeast is a microorganism, a tiny living thing, that feeds on sugar. As yeast grows, it multiplies, producing bubbles of gas. This gas makes bread dough rise.

Something to try

Grow yeast at different temperatures

You will need:
sugar, plain flour, dried yeast, two glass jam jars, two small plastic bowls, cold and warm water, a waterproof marker, a watch.

In each jar, carefully mix together two teaspoons of sugar, two tablespoons of flour, four tablespoons of warm water, and two teaspoons of dried yeast until a smooth dough is formed. Mark the height of the dough mixture on the side of each jar, using a waterproof marker. Stand the first jar in a bowl of cool water, and stand the second in a bowl of water from the hot tap, which is about 122°F (50°C). Check the height of each dough mixture at three-minute intervals for thirty minutes. In which jar does the dough rise the most? See what happens if you leave a third dough mixture in a bowl filled with ice cubes.

At what temperature does yeast grow best?

P.S. Try the dough experiment at a higher temperature. Ask an adult to help you stand a jar in a bowl of very hot water. What happens and why?

Warm temperatures also make bacteria and molds grow quickly. If you leave food in a warm place for too long, mold and bacteria may soon grow on it. If you keep food cool in the refrigerator, bacteria cannot grow so quickly, and the food stays fresh longer.

Changes through heat

When we bake bread or cake, the soft batter is hardened by the high temperature. A similar thing happens when clay is fired. Clay, used to make pots and bricks, is fired in an oven, or kiln, at 1,832°F (1,000°C). It looks very different after it has been fired.

All materials exist in one of three forms: as a solid, a liquid, or a gas. We call these the three states of matter. When materials are heated or cooled, many will change from one state to another.

Many materials change from solids into liquids when heated, and back again when cooled. Gold has a melting point of 1,947.2°F (1,064°C). Liquid gold can be made into gold ingots or bars. Iron will melt if it is heated to 2,804°F (1,540°C) in a furnace. Liquid iron can be poured into molds, where it cools and hardens. Tools, gates, and girders are made in this way.

If you cool water down to 32°F (0°C), it will turn into solid ice. As soon as the temperature rises above 32°F (0°C), the ice will begin to melt.

Many liquids change into gases when heated. Water boils at 212°F (100°C). As it does, some of the water changes into water vapor, a gas that seems to disappear into the air. There is water vapor in the air around us. We can change it back into a liquid by cooling it down.

Something to try

Collect some water vapor

You will need: a glass, a mirror, some hot water, a bowl, rubber gloves.

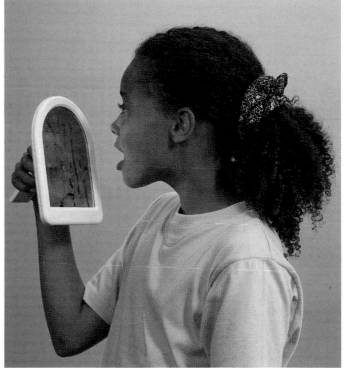

Place the glass and the mirror in a refrigerator for one hour. Ask an adult to fill a bowl with hot water. Wear a rubber glove and hold the cold glass over the water. Watch for droplets of water to collect on the glass.

You can also collect water vapor from the air you breathe out. Breathe out onto the cold mirror.

P.S. Find out the temperature (in °F and °C) at which liquid iron and mercury will turn into gases.

Hot and cold — then and now

No one knows when humans first used fire to keep warm. Prehistoric people probably discovered it by accident thousands of years ago. Over the centuries, wood, charcoal, and coal have all been used for heating.

During the Industrial Revolution in the nineteenth century, huge amounts of coal were used to run machines and provide heat. Today, we burn coal, gas, and oil to make electricity. Electricity can power heating systems that keep us warm and air conditioning units and fans that keep us cool.

Coal, gas, and oil are fossil fuels, which means they were formed from the bodies of plants and animals that died millions of years ago. Today, as we burn more and more fossil fuels, we are damaging our environment. As the fuels burn, they release gases, including a lot of carbon dioxide. The extra carbon dioxide in our atmosphere traps heat that is causing a slight rise in Earth's temperature. This is called the "greenhouse effect." If the world becomes warmer by even a few degrees, some places could suffer severe changes as a result. This could lead to flooding and drought, which would destroy farmland and homes.

Earth's supply of fossil fuels will run out one day. Scientists are looking for new ways to provide heat and energy. One of these is to use nuclear power, but even this has serious disadvantages. It is important that we try to discover other ways of producing the energy future generations will need.

Many people are interested in using sources of energy such as the Sun, wind, and water. Modern windmills use turbines to make electricity. You can see the turbines in this photograph of a "wind farm." Solar panels are also sometimes used. These glass panels collect the Sun's rays and convert their energy into electricity. If these sources of energy can be used efficiently, perhaps they will provide fuel for the future.

Index

For a free color catalog describing Gareth Stevens' list of high-quality books, call 1-800-542-2595 (USA) or 1-800-461-9120 (Canada). Gareth Stevens' Fax: (414) 225-0377.

Library of Congress Cataloging-in-Publication Data

Walpole, Brenda.
  Temperature/by Brenda Walpole; photographs by Chris Fairclough; illustrations by Dennis Tinkler.
    p. cm — (Measure up with science)
  Includes bibliographical references and index.
  Summary: Discusses the elements of temperature, from sunlight and thermometers to water vapor and insulation, and examines ways of measuring temperature.
  ISBN 0-8368-1363-4
  1. Temperature—Juvenile literature.
2. Temperature measurements—Study and teaching—Activity programs—Juvenile literature. [1. Temperature.] I. Fairclough, Chris, ill. II. Tinkler, Dennis, ill. III. Title. IV. Series: Walpole, Brenda. Measure up with science.
QC271.4.W35   1995
536—dc20   95-21854

This edition first published in 1995 by
Gareth Stevens Publishing
1555 North RiverCenter Drive, Suite 201
Milwaukee, Wisconsin 53212, USA

This edition © 1995 by Gareth Stevens, Inc. Original edition published in 1995 by A & C Black (Publishers) Ltd., 35 Bedford Row, London WC1R 4JH. © 1995 A & C Black (Publishers) Ltd. Additional end matter © 1995 by Gareth Stevens, Inc.

Acknowledgements
Photographs by Chris Fairclough, except for: p. 4 (t) Lifefile; p. 8 Michael Holford; p. 9 Ann Ronan Picture Library; p. 11 Malcolm Fielding, Johnson Matthey Plc/Science Photo Library; pp. 12 (t), 15 (b), 28 (b) Mary Evans Picture Library; p. 17 (t) Hulton-Deutsch Collection; pp. 17 (b), 26 (b), 29 ZEFA; p. 18 Electricity Association; p. 20 (b) Ed Barber; p. 23 (b) Frank Lane Picture Agency.

Printed in Mexico
1 2 3 4 5 6 7 8 9 99 98 97 96 95